The Good News

ROB A. MACKENZIE is author of *The Opposite of Cabbage* and two pamphlets, *Fleck and the Bank* and *The Clown of Natural Sorrow*. He writes poetry, reviews and criticism, is reviews editor at *Magma Poetry* magazine, and blogs at Surroundings.

The Good News

by

ROB A. MACKENZIE

SALT

CROMER

PUBLISHED BY SALT PUBLISHING
12 Norwich Road, Cromer, Norfolk NR27 0AX
All rights reserved

Salt Publishing 2013

Printed in Great Britain by the MPG Books Group, Bodmin and King's Lynn

Typeset in Paperback 9 / 13

ISBN 978 1 907773 42 6 hardback

1 3 5 7 9 8 6 4 2

for Alyssa

Contents

Acknowledgements

Some of these poems or earlier versions of them appeared in: *Gutter, Magma, New Walk, Rising, Shearsman* and *Silk Road Review*.

Bladerunner was selected for the Scottish Poetry Library's online anthology, *Best Scottish Poems 2011* (http://bit.ly/JiKiYE)

The Organist was commissioned for the Hidden Door Arts Festival, Edinburgh, October 2010.

On the Willow Branches is a translation of Salvatore Quasimodo's Alle Fronde dei Salici, from his collection *Giorno dopo Giorno* (1947), and was published in *The FSG Book of Twentieth Century Italian Poetry*, ed. Geoffrey Brock (Farrar, Straus and Giroux, New York, 2012).

A.M. Meda, Jeweller, is a translation of Davide Rondoni's A. M. Meda orifice artigiano, from the collection, *Il Bar Del Tempo* (Ugo Guanda Editore, Parma, 1999)

Thanks to A.B. Jackson, Roddy Lumsden and Andrew Philip for their help and support during the writing of this collection, and to Chris, Jen and all at Salt.

The Good News

The Good News

I.

The Lingua Franca Happy Hour

1.

Sunday Morning

'Cloquet hated reality but realized it was still the only place to get a good steak'

WOODY ALLEN

The New Year headlines are retro. Graves
open and close like coinless fish-mouths.
The traffic police survive on fish fingers:
cod-and-tattie coffins, frozen stiffs.

I'm trying to deliver my frozen self.
A neighbour punches a hole in the wall,
wails that he's on *Songs of Praise*.
That's too much reality for my life.

In church, I range from point to point.
My sermon's like a marathon speeded up,
Bible in one hand, New York in the other:
Lou Reed spitting out the Septuagint.

Someone has painted SLOW on the road
and witnessed a rush of broken exhausts.
Why bother? – a little bread, a little wine,
the rest processed for the quick and dead.

An Angry Queen Tours
The Royal Mile

So, Bar Whiski, is it? And kids are *kidz*?
Let us dumb down and dull the will to live.
A mind, both Kailyard and Etonian,
rebrands the languid natives as 'Creatives',
the businesses as panegyric souvenirs:
Fantastic Scotland, Prestige Scotland, The Real
Scots Shop, Scotland's matchstick Parliament –
each inflames my erstwhile cobbled colony.
All cobblers! A lick of tartan paint will neither
glamorise your cowed interior
nor free your brio. I spit on your effeminate
cultural zing. I spit on the Starbucks-adjunct
tagged as the 'Scottish Poetry Library':
a monstrous regiment of Delphic upstarts
and barbarians no self-respecting Duke
or Marmaduke would rank as literate.
I spit on one untutored rhymer's plinth –

   'and blythly gar auld care gae by
      wi' blinkit and wi' bleering eye' –

I will not be hoodwinked! No arcane wisdom
sings from a dead tongue. The living hit
The Cannon's Gut, Bank Bar, The Killing Station,
and line up for the lingua franca happy hour's
chilled, effulgent, lime-scented fright.
I spit in your stone heart, your wart
of Midlothian, your sullen tramwreck hurt
that beats a crash and boom to The World's End.

I spit on the destiny of Scone. I spit on
your castle, your puny cardboard ruin. The rain
spits, I spit at the rain: imported English-
rain and Scot-rain, equivocally split.
As clouds swing low across the stars, the spires,
the spilt milk and the penitence-in-waiting,
I catch the Baguette Express from Cafe Vivo
down to the raffish haunts of Holyrood,
brandish a hairbrush microphone and stir
the living statues with public blandishments.

Blade Runner

Tell me once more of your conversion,
your decluttered ambition to mine
a pure theology by candlestub.
Take me to the back street barber
to chop my priestly beard, and then let's
split up. It's too late for me to bugger
off to the Episcopalians and become
a bishop, which is all you ever wanted
through the jumble sale years,
when asking 'What would Descartes do?'
was your answer to everything.
I will save my chin hair in this leather
wallet labelled *Relics of a Sinner*,
ready made for the bells and smells
of futuristic Edinburgh – cat-calling
choirs rattling pails after closing time
among winged taxis and unfinished
tramlines, like a cut of *Blade Runner*
directed only by CCTV cameras –
a confusing place to be religious.

The Five Thousand

Bullet sculptures veneered in fishnet appropriate for
the zeitgeist caught his lusty eye, which explains why

the ironist arrived late for the miracle, twelve baskets
returning stink to the air from which had formed

all that remained of holiness, while professional fudgers
battled to square myth with physics, body with bread,

faith with sceptic tongues which had not tasted yet believed
themselves entitled to a proof before being guillotined

to give everyone a little peace. The hour's bestseller was
Biggles: The Teenage Years, autobiography thinly disguised

as fiction, the story of an era historical revisionists claimed
may never have happened in the same sense that miracles

happen or afterlives are gatecrashed. Facts were marshalled,
a dumb movie guaranteed late entry to their popular insight.

What became popular was the debunking, the ironist's brilliant
unbalanced brain doubting everything but his own doubt

or distraction. 'There are no possible clarities,' he became
certain, disturbed slightly by this fundamental tenet's lack

of ambiguity, as if a defining sign had misdirected outcomes
without his consent and left him in a mounting huff.

Without Content

The shallow end, the perfect place to start
thrashing out a front crawl, ponderous butterfly,
   triggering the deep

to answer with a thin Olympian ripple lost
among the counterblast of rule-breaking
   dive bombers:

dangerous, edgy for a second, like comedians
testing taboos, quickly retreating to the spent
   contentment of laughter,

polycathartic laughter, laughter ill-at-ease
with itself. A new generation of laughter
   jounces around

the Victorian walls, resplendent in fifty shades
of phlegm; my one available flight from hilarity
   a dip underwater,

eyes shut, regular stroke count from breadth
to breadth, monotonous rhythm snuffing out
   constant barking merriment

over all measure of pain in bars, bedrooms
and poolsides. The new comedy is old banter,
   a sense of humour

its weapon. I better stay under. It has been
ninety-seven breadths since my last regression
　　into grinning at nothing.

My name is Mr. Emily Dickinson. I hate alcopops.
I am a swim king, an alchemist, a Calvinholic.
　　Don't think I'm not serious.

Locus-a-Non

I have taken up poetry, language stripped
of bare essentials until only the stylised
detritus remains – involuntary Oulipo:

adverbs, latinates, exclamation marks,
ill-advised semi-colons; canonical
formlessness the single permitted anxiety

of influence. Like all poets, I am employed
as locus-a-non, leaning on brooms, accepting
praise long after the sweepers have gone.

A Scottish Cent(o)ury

This is a difficult land. Here things miscarry,
fates get their yarn in a twist,
but greet, an' in your tears ye'll drown.
Jings! But it's laughable, tae,
the permanence of the young men
filled with synthetic joy,
remembering smoke and flowerless slum
lit up like a paper lantern,
their laughter a mist in my ears.
I think, quiet Midnight, that the sun will rise
which lay in a ditch, its mouth full of dying fires
blown in blown out again
cold and luminous like a moon,
a death wha's licht slocks me.
Acquiring is what's easy, relinquishing, what's hard.
A great place and its people are not renewed lightly
in time's grace, the grace of change,
a change of more than silhouette.
O knives, forks and spoons, fulfil yourselves!
History has made you slaves to short-arsed curers
who buy peripheral history to confirm some malcontents in
                                                    palaces,
put worms to work, and moles to mark
every simple terror of a single brain of fish
as out of the dark they swing:
'OK, you got this far, you passed the test,
au revoir to you ma petite sardine.'
The committee of unthinkable thoughts
are ringing constantly with their questions:

how much mystery we need to make a world moment by
                                        moment escaping
how we undervalue all earlier anxieties.
With habitual disregard for public safety
I twine the past through my fingers:
hits mizzerlessness, da marginalia, da element o winder.
Every day its being shifts with
morning's levitation over hills and cold rain.
What should we fly from Scotland's drizzlements?
kilts, skirts, troosers, shorts?
New Gen and their ad men?
sweet gentle modest lightness?
a wee hairy dog with two wee eyes?
murdered fish suppers?
cigarettes, their spent ends?
Let those who can still read, read the signs,
be upstanding. Now: let us raise the fucking *tone*:
somewhere between a tenor and an alto, this rosé voice –
master of the 30-length stanza, Olympian,
blind drunk from politeness –
relapses into patterns of favourite self-pitying sentiments,
plunges into the déjà vu of a phlegm-skied twilight
down some Scottish plughole:
a darkness that grows
ready to hypnotise with drills –
a mouth-watering prospect for the damned.
The road to hell is paved with clichés, friend.
Three goldfish gleam in the pupil appraising
a future lit by bridges and the burning
Big Barn of the Gaelic Resurrection,

all but real for a moment, then
a crumpled heaven,
a furnace made of tiny fishhooks,
a head lickin holes where limbs once were,
a drift of greens and reds that make no sense.
Is that no enough for the Scots Lords tae cry, enuff's enuff,
turn a fresh eye on this outworn frame?
May we make of it something else!
Night downs its curtain on the show:
tar boils out of the toffeed sleepers
and a voice from elsewhere whispers, *He is risen,*
threaded on time
like the continual rain,
the distant Latin chanting of a train.
Time to bite on a spring onion,
botox our frownliness,
eat avocados with apostle spoons.
We stare back over decades
spliced into bars of an old wheel
about to crack the darkness
that sight imposes on the world.
It takes a rare person to look through stones to the other side
believing this compact rolling ball could be restored, maybe,
                                 maybe, maybe.

We see nothing but fog,
a struck match,
a spirit released, a loss,
and somewhere, someone singing flat,
'Dinna be glaikit, dinna be ower smert.'
We set our compass tae a fremmit airt,

tour the sodden carbrain underpasses
through the needle's eye
on the far side of the water,
look hard into the deep, unshouldered blue.
And the sea, the sea takes care of everything,
as hungry as the flame below
the years, the tears, the dead;
we dat koort da storm's upstierin
expect deliverance in smoke,
essays of soot,
words that sound each arc of hurt.
We leap bareback through the rainbow's hoop,
not an escape itself but its fine surprise
partly revealed and partly veiled,
our wishes bright against a sullen sky.

On the Willow Branches

Salvatore Quasimodo

And we, how could we have sung,
with a foreign foot pressed on our heart,
among the dead littering the piazzas
on grass brittle with ice, over the lamblike
crying of children, over the black howl
of the mother who stumbled upon her son
crucified on a telegraph pole?
On the willow branches, as offerings,
even our harps were suspended,
and rocked gently in the mourning wind.

The Point

The point is to repeat. To repeat the point,
the point is worth repeating, even if not:
we need to stick by the manual, even if useless,
to talk about how we think the things we've thought.

The point is worth repeating, even if not
worth retweeting. We cannot trust ourselves
to talk about how we think the things we've thought.
Our independence, our politics, our fitting demise

are not worth retweeting. We cannot trust ourselves
to train a parrot. We need experts to refine
our independence, our politics, our fitting demise,
like the Prime Minister and his unlikeable sidekick.

To train a parrot, we need experts to refine
our received pronunciation. Repeat after me,
'We like the Prime Minister and his unlikeable sidekick' –
not to sound desperate, but sing fortissimo, with comedy

in received pronunciation. Repeat after me,
as the point *is* to repeat, to repeat the point,
not to sound desperate. Sing fortissimo, with comedy,
we need to stick by the manual, even if useless.

Tippexed Speeches on Scottish Independence

there is a danger of thinking of Scotland
        recruiting ground for
                the future Conservative Party

I'm not here to make a case
        the reason I make the case is
                I am a classic case

I am proud to be
        like so many others, I am proud to be
                safer, not just because
        our tentacles reach

we're richer, because
        we're fairer. We are saving thousands
                that we and others take for granted

I also understand why people
        want a Scotland where more people own
                where more people keep more
        where businesses can

I passionately believe
        the people of Scotland
                believe that
        which is why I'm ready for the

11 Nick Clegg, Spring Conference, 2012

I want the Scottish people to have
Scottish affairs

Salmond wants to
I want to

he says this is
I say it is

he wants to
I want us to

it is our job, as liberals

I may be Deputy Prime Minister
I am as much of a radical as ever

III ED MILIBAND, JUNE 2012

       one part of the United Kingdom
  I want to reflect

          we should also talk
we have been too nervous to talk

       we must talk
  because people are talking

       people like Jeremy Clarkson
shrug their shoulders

   cut off from the rest of Britain

IV ALEX SALMOND, OCTOBER 2011

people cheering us on
a great asset

        we govern
        we have governed
        we have sheltered
        we have frozen
        we have held down
        we have abolished
        we have tried to control
        we have a prices and incomes policy
        we govern well
        we are the SNP

our focus is on
John Swinney and his
gas for the next 40 years

        we will export
        we shall ensure
        we have created the Scottish Futures
        we face a winter
        we already have the best heating
        we have invested
        we have expanded

the Tories call it a Big Society
I call it no society at all

    we are a party with a mission
    we shall prevail

Thirteen

'*And all over again something begins*
That will end so staggeringly, so unresistingly'

DURS GRUNBEIN

i.

Once again the Nihilists are spreading
breadcrumbs around the kitchen floor
    to make a point or, rather, demonstrate
that progress built on optimistic
    droppings from an evening's staple
only feeds your desire for luxury.
    They are right and being right,
to them, is agony. Their debugged version
    of truth hypes the dreadful hoover
mouthing over bacteria-rich linoleum,
    fuels anger at bankers, fresh blunders
with lottery numbers, excessive
    prayers mercifully left unanswered.

ii.

Pale bottled sauce similar to others
you have stewed in earthenware –
   garlic, basil, cream, small polymorphous
chunks from a supermarket tray,
   blended until rootless, chameleonic.
You might as well drift shipless
   and starcold on the Mediterranean dark,
reminiscing deep-fried haggis, the big
   tartan bang, embarrassing moments
in country dancing history: folklore
   this tiny global moment treats as if
curiously antique, whose value
   lies in the tearful, uneducated eye.

iii.

The BBC website warns of sleet heading south
from where you are, quietly curtaining
   the single glazed window and unpacking
fresh subtext from each update overload:
   How do you paint an aeroplane? New incurable
nodding disease. Why so many lack belief
   in Timbuktu. The complex world of dating
the disabled. Strictly on a need-to-
   know basis, you'd bypass the lot, but sense
the hobgoblin of syncretic diversion
   might be tapping at your skull. You bend to
the brimmed infobath and the day
   drains a glass largely without you in it.

iv.

The mudslide within your bowels requires
a vial of peppermint oil and no further hint
  of contentment. Simmer, purify and smear:
stressed warts drop on the third day
  beneath the titymalli's milky sap. Pound cabbage
with aged lard and fry it on the scars.
  Do not trust a wondercut, the shepherd's purse
or white hellebore, as Dr Chancellor implores,
  but peonies aflame guarantee a daily shag
before a storm. Sweet basil checks tabloidache
  or scorpion attack. At daybreak the sow thistle
may be sucked – let it be when the moon
  enters Capricorn. No evil will hunt you down.

v.

The puddle at the roadside is waiting to be
tossed your way – a fallen cloud,
    occupied lasso strung out and at the mercy
of human traffic, as you are, posing before
    a mobile phone like a diva, tracking
a bus that seems due permanently
    five minutes late. Time has left the smashed
shelter, you realise, to timetables:
    a parallel hypothesis where the rules apply
like Switzerland, or Sinai before the long
    slide to earth. If you were Moses, you'd stir
the puddle with a staff until it rose like
    a highlight, slowmo, to meet you head on.

vi.

Alone in the hatchback, you get to thinking
about the vacant seats, vast boot space
    for spanner and oilcan, how the temporary
lights make time for cramming thoughts
    into deodorized air. How loud they sound
without anyone to hear them, brash
    as potholes, singing along with radio jingles
independently as if you didn't count,
    sliding under seatbelts and expropriating
gum from drawers. They leave you
    the wheel for company, they find solace
in one another and refuse to budge for
    a woman you seem to know, with baggage.

II.

Claw snatched from the window, show tune
flatlined from the outhouse, basil leaves curling,
    your left eye burning up
the Paracetamol's bid to dull all sense
    of feeling. Every day you feel outraged
about nothing, increasingly aware of how far
    contentment will go to keep you
chained to her bones. Today you turn up
    five habits to quit for happiness:
criticism, control, complaint, excuses, expectations,
    without which you'd be happy, bland
and unbearable. The claw is back, scratching at
    the window, your head immediately clear.

VIII

Develop interests: housework, the sick or elderly,
a hobby that involves the use of hands.
   Try hands-off thinking, shitstorm solutions.
Happy people accept suffering, ask them for ideas.
   Blue lights and blue shirts produce euphoria.
Religious incense relaxes test mice.
   A long walk is a step in the right direction.
Overeating delays feelings which ginger and broccoli
   swiftly air. Lemon and onion, chop and sniff.
Examine expectations, adjust for despair.
   Read and repeat, 'I can't read minds.'
Approximate a smile. Remove 'depressed' from
   your vocabulary. Substitute 'low moods'.

IX.

They kept even contempt beyond arm's length,
sent a terrified office junior to receive
    the petition and, in the House of Commons,
only the unauthorised jesters (Skinner, Benn, Cook)
    shook your hand. This was '88, you'd marched
six hundred miles of tarmac for one man:
    terrorist (Order of the Burning Necklace), killer
of democracy. They'd all flown to Johannesburg,
    tanked up on Grenache and safari snaps. Weren't
the blacks so loyal, so colourful? From 2012,
    Odessey & Oracle full blast, the microwave rings time
on flower power, on the aggregate of gestures;
    your nails dig into flesh, almost draw blood.

x.

Events chafed at history's border
while, within, dates were being
    forgotten as they were recorded,
names proclaimed and marked
    marginàl or absent, such as yours
whatever it was when, from some
    hermetical firmament, smoke
pining for its flame thinned to
    a low horizon and became
your signature hint, imaginatively
    silent catchphrase: history in
the unmaking, your erasure
    as indelible masterstroke.

xi.

Hard, you assume, to avoid the falling log,
hidden dip, young men with cracked faces,
    harried and joyridden, crashed out on corners,
hungry for a light. Or was that a fight?
You have staked your life on baiting the slant
ladder's invitation, its tottering paintpot,
    the cracked mirror hung in the hallway,
the thirteenth note. But who's counting?
Someone, you assume, despite the unassuming
gait you cultivate – the desultory slump
    from luck to lack, faith to fate – a speculator
with metal detector, without a prayer,
    buying up the latest house of cards.

XII.

Where prayer, not as request but as a step
toward confluence, one of infinite
    patternless manoeuvrings – the crisscrossed
highways of fish or dissipated jet stream
    pooled in the camera lens as aftershock,
as once-was, beyond tense and proof text,
    pure sky and ocean, blue and black –
discovers itself falling short
    of expectation, webbed within the mass
digital exchange of wireless hearts
    and minds unable to contain
their own mystery, you enter the shroud,
    enter the words unpronounced, incognito.

Hands unclasped, you pass the cooling towers
and slag heaps south of York, from the A1
   like sooty trampolines, offspring of a billion
high tar cigarettes, burnt-out cemetery
   ashes to ashes . . . and yet the newborn
lambs dance like marionettes in a Spring field,
   awkward skins lumber into calfhood,
two llamas act surprised to see you
   from scrubland east of Duddo, west of Spittal
. . . dust to dust, bodily resurrection: faith's
   unapologetic paradox: confusion, mystery,
contradiction, not dogma or assent, are the draw;
   the bridge of sorrows its blind summit.

II.
Autistic Variations

'So many gods rioting around one head'

SENECA

Health Check

The chromosomes were grey oblongs except the fourteenth right –
    a cartoon hunchback in the rain.

'Can't be from my side,' Anne joked, but when recalled to test
    for Down's, we remembered

its broken umbrella, the burden it carried on behalf of all
    beautiful flaws.

Returning to our minds, Milan the night before the positive
    pregnancy test:

supersize margaritas and fizzing thimblefuls of slammed
    Tequila beating out

cells from our inconceivable fetus's non-existent brain;
    and dream-visitations

from my ancestor, nineteenth century mathematics professor,
    who pressed

his Habsburg chin against a dry stone dyke whenever
    human contact threatened

his reclusive equilibrium; from Anne's pedigree, a second cousin
    forced to wear

wig and crown, to pound a gavel over a house of dolls
    and remove the guilty

heads with a cheese knife; my great-great grandmother,
    shopkeeper and sage,

who claimed direct lineage from a 13th century Scottish king –
    it all counts as expenditure

when accounting for blame, though at the birth we tallied
    only relief that everything

was *normal*. What hypocrites! as if we embraced normality
    or believed it possible.

The Tower

Gurgle, babble,
a current of words –

utterance fluid
as memory,
as definition –

you spilled downriver
toward the expanse
crowding beyond
the cataract,

then turned,
a dictionary
erasing itself,
swimming upstream
back to Babel.

Helpless, we consulted
useless books
from our crackling tower.

Torino in Furs

We persevered with mismatched floor tiles and *Rai Due*
    in our claustrophobic flat;

through the walls the unmistakable sound of Italian
    Teletubbies and Sesame Street,

and across the courtyard the young engineer's CD:
    Learn English

from 1950s BBC Newscasters, phrases like 'I'm sorry,
    this is not *your* shower,

it is *my* shower,' decadence we brushed against otherwise
    only in the gelateria

of imagination. From antiseptic pillars and ladies furred
    for autumn strolls,

the city thrived on appearance and threat: nearly everyone
    drove a Fiat,

not usually from choice. We prammed you to the Cafe Zelli
    and on your tongue

ritually dabbed espresso, as if this could consecrate you
    bilingual more readily

than daytrips to the swing park, where you unflaggingly
    cold-shouldered any child

who approached with a 'Ciao!' Not that it happened often;
    even the Torinese

tots seemed to know that alien kids were best observed
    with suitable tact,

that playing among and playing with could appear the same
    to untrained eyes:

a whole city with Asperger Syndrome, which is perhaps why
    it began to feel like home.

The Synagogue

Those bright winter mornings, the sky
high over Piazzetta Primo Levi,
I'd buy croissants from the bakery,
refuse the advance of the elderly
Albanian shemales, and wheel your pram
past the synagogue's twenty-four hour
police guard, who'd smile and nod,
machine guns trained on me daily
in case one day I showed them a clean
pair of heels and left you to explode.

But Not Hyperlexic

We read, you watched, and when the time felt right
    you made your mark

on nursery, reading a book to an astonished teacher
    from start to finish,

aged three. How long you feigned an inability
    and how you learned

the intricate decoding from sign to sound,
    we never learned,

although we learned the word, *hyperlexic*, and why
    it didn't apply to you,

and more likely words coding intractable conditions
    in root positive.

Half in hope and half with the desperate aspirations
    we despised

in parents of young tennis prospects, we imagined
    you a savant

decades on: the recitation of Juvenal's complete works
    backwards in Latin

to a packed Royal Albert Hall and no one thinking
    dead language

a waste of time. But your intelligence was reserved for
    a different world;

this one demanded contact on first name terms,
    eye to eye,

to read its script. You feigned interest in learning
    the pointless dialogue.

The Doors

Our new Victorian house
had too many doors.

You complained about getting lost
between attic and pantry.

The doors all looked the same:
some opening, others shutting.

Sometimes we were the doors
you opened and shut
    opened and shut.

Progress of a Kind

The old obsessions recycle themselves as fresh
    claims to originality

twice a second: indistinguishably, *Big Society*
    see-saws with *There is no*

such thing as society, soundbites barbed enough
    to enact

a persistent hailstorm thirty years apart over some
    ex-mining town

moonlighting as a life-size social history exhibit
    no one visits

halfway between identical Little Chefs, plastic seats
    bent out of shape

by immensity and bad posture – arses for courses –
    like craters

evidencing ancient collisions on uninhabited moons.
    Each small impact

implies progress, journeys that mark time in passing,
    that value us

no more than the tarmac values the love, passion
    and intelligence

we parade like roadkill down this lowland motorway,
     proud of our speedy

ability to marshal facts for optimal emotional effect:
     the lonely distance

separating planets to the nearest inch, the tiny breach
     we hatch within

a light year, my childhood fascination with astronomy
     echoed in your command

of solar system data, unearthly long-range hearing
     and shuttle fantasies:

ice-light craft shuddering through mercurial terrain,
     resolute and free

of clamour for distinction, to Mercury's double-edged
     sure-fire climate.

Hyper Emotion

The biggest misconception:

that it steals emotion
and compassion
for others or on behalf of others;

that it feels
metallic when, in fact,
it softens too easily:

the inconstant fluorescent
light's invisible flicker
sees it running
from a bright superstore;

a television picture
pixel by pixel by pixel by pixel,
a single human voice's
overwhelming
warmth,
sees it running
for the unwelcome
terror of a crowd.

Routine

Your hot waterbottle is liturgical, the latest ritual
    we need to follow

before you fall asleep; waterbottle by your pillow,
    waterglass on the wardrobe,

a drawn-out watershed, which elongates in silence
    or hours of to and fro –

any excuse to stay awake and see the constellations
    demythologise the dark

psalm of sky. You aim to arrange stray mysteries
    the more unruly

the rules become, the more illegible and cracked
    a face appears

if reading it is required. But you are more difficult
    for us to read

than Proust translated into sixty-seven languages
    or gossip mags packed

with undistinguished stars, who span the earth
    like water, logged

but hard to account for, with depths and limitations
    resolutely immeasurable.

The Trouble

The trouble with me is the fog that enters the picture.
The trouble with the picture is that no one is able to draw it.
The trouble with drawing is that monkeys have fingers of tar.
The trouble with tar is the same as the trouble with you.
The trouble with you is the invisible side of the road.
The trouble with the road is the roadkill learning Turkish.
The trouble with Turkey is that lovers are busy with lobster.
The trouble with lobster is their surreal sense of humour.
The trouble with humour is the pain of saying what I want to.
The trouble with saying is the person whose being is said.
The trouble with being is the same as the trouble with love.
The trouble with love is the fear of saying what I want to.
The trouble with want is the same as the trouble with you.
The trouble with you is the same as the trouble with me.
The trouble with me is my surreal sense of humour.
The trouble with sense is the fog that enters the picture.

Consequential Egg

You prefer the murk of details to the vision complete,
  incident to plot,

incidental to mainstream. You like books for hilarity
  halfway down page 17,

oblivious to consequence. You don't care who lived
  happily ever after

or how a mystery is solved, and closure is important
  only for the satisfaction

of completion. All this is why, on the number 12
  heading for your ninth

birthday party, I eavesdrop on the conversation
  behind us –

how a conceptual artist assembled a giant egg
  from ten thousand

eggshell pieces – and imagine you building an egg
  from splinters,

each selected according to your personal aesthetic,
  fascinated by the fit

they make, the gaps and incongruities, building
  patiently for weeks

until an egg the size of a bus wobbles on a tiny cup.
How does it end?

An ending would be a betrayal. Already you have
begun the next egg.

III.

Human Manoeuvre

Experience

In five years I rode more aircraft than my parents
    in a lifetime

and where they took me, beyond the generic
    runways and ruins

some call *experience*, cannot be found in atlas,
    flight path

or rough guide to spiritual competence. Every
    dose of reality

leaves the tang of absence. The moment
    I leave a place,

I taste it in the next bright thing: each capital
    city a mere simile

for others, each neon facade disguising the dark
    ache within

the hearts and minds of Human Resources
    boffins employed

to keep bulbs blazing through the nightshift.
    If that shadow

over the lung looks sinister, they polish it
    until it gleams;

they hang a sign, FIT FOR LIGHT WORK,
    around my shoulders

until I drop, and they deny the existence
    of paths to Sheol,

shady arenas and grey areas, cataracts as
    windows to the soul,

while all units under their care are confirmed
    'fantastically normal'

and everyone gets along fantastic normally
    in spite of everything.

The Organist

Sunday morning, I pass by
roadside thistles (what blossoming
beards they have, what holy beards),
and think of the organist's beefy
fingers and bear-solemn mouth
just as she thinks of me,
my headful of crumbs and water
still to spill its way to wine,
sermon coiled in my breast pocket
like a pre-charmed snake.
She anticipates the hesitancy
jarred within my speech
(what words and roses, what
flowery words) and makes mistakes
in sympathy, readies the choir
to sing like ducks when I arrive.
The organist, chillingly advanced,
could do with a lesson or two
in emotion, on playing grumpily.
Anything so the notes sound less
like mass market kitchen tiles.
She shuts her eyes, and tries.
My mind is her bootleg cathedral
and 'All Things Bright and Beautiful'
beetles down my aisles – the temporal
lobes – hymns my journey here:
weeds, stubble, drunks, the hanging
garden, scorched earth, road signs
batting by like clouds over pavements
glass-showered: beauty

umbilical, incomplete, corrosive.
She has given of her best,
I see that. I see it so close up
her quizzical scowl is blurred.
I feel it, her music from the heart,
but I do not feel enough.

Soundings

Ululate, my angels, with pie-eyed choirs
after the derby match, pained animals
stretched from traps, mouths muffling
in pillows the usual breaches of trust.

Your perfect harmonies no longer strike
a chord. Low level sound surrounds me:
milk in a froth, tills opening and closing
to Radiohead in this Costa Cafe, where you,

my angels, tap laptops, weep quietly
in Spanish into cold latte, or bunch up
between earphones in a corner, whispering.
I can't hear you. Pump up the volume.

A. M. Meda, Jeweller

Davide Rondoni

Your rooms are pure gold, Mario,
in such disorder,
                shredded paper, scraps
of metal, wax polish,
pencilled drafts,
plates chipped along the edges.
                       You make rings,
bracelets, you separate
light from laminate, capture
pale blue brilliance in sapphire.
There are beakers, an old
broken bicycle, a table
spread with pencils,
with jars –
        it's over, your ugly apartment
has sunk, a Titanic, into Milan.
You are tight-lipped
even in the telling of your mother's
long and terrible death.
                 It was an execution, you say,
she screamed in these rooms
where now I survey jewels.
It lasted a month, without respite.
They are pure gold, Mario, these idle
walls of your gold-shaping laboratory,
                    they are pearls
your tired Lombardy vowels,
they are lyric poems
the swallows flying in the courtyard –
it is pure gold, this, your motionless

[60]

April,
        and the silence, Mario,
    it doesn't go away.

The Shadow

Darkness has no shadow, unlike Death, who floats one a centimetre greater
than our expanding universe, always with her entourage of shivering
light to buff cheekbones to optimal effect like an insubordinately
alive Rita Hayworth – and what a shadow she had! No end
and the only way out a step after step into darkness.
By her last film, she had to request a fresh take
for every line, memory so much confined
to the moment at hand and all behind
and ahead shadowless, obvious and
lost and, standing at the corner,
Death with her gleaming red
wheelbarrow, gardening
implements and
chickenloads
shining her
torch into
Rita's
eye.

Nocturnes

stars at 5pm

    sleet
the eyes of darkness

       an ice cream van
           woos the night's
        tone-deaf ear

     in concert
the lash of tongues
sills' whistling lips
spouses around a kitchen table
  exchanging ringtones

       the drum of unwanted
longing in human skin

#2

evening wears me
like a shellsuit
moth-eaten but serviceable

from lawns snowmen
flash hermeneutic
on emerging slush

outside decorations
a must this year
every garden has its North Pole
electric kitsch
bells on the gatepost

cult accessory of the party season
meccano Christmas tree

Iran's president blesses television
in Jesus' name
a cold snap

grottos expand in distant capitals
bombs unveil horizons

the bus shelter hoarding
Scratch Cards Make Great Gifts

#3

a beautiful busker calls
'. . . you're my wonderwall'

    or perhaps   wallflower
                   Windy Miller
                     winterwilly stroking
                       the shores of Lake Windermere

    no wind
or obvious wonder

        for one night only
     midnight's smoking jacket slowly

                                unbuttoning

       nightmare loop
   Margaret Thatcher jiggling on top
    shouting, 'No milk for you!'

still working the 27th floor
city boys gamble
      someone else's life
          and lose

  the usual novelties
    repeat themselves

a helicopter leap is the new
marriage registry office
parachute
or no parachute
morning will fall

#4

conservative preachers
whip up snowmen
against the blacks

to ice, pebble and carrot
inspired by the wind's unholy
spirited whine
hatred in the clogged gut

doors open to the deep
nightclub funk

perfume sweat blood
imperceptible migration

snow thins
to sleet

one way ticket from heat
to hell

not only the melting shape God
in their own image

#5

evening service

   fawnsuit with glasses and ruby earring
                        looms from the vestibule

tightless girls
      cold-shoulder the drifting organ

         who needs ecstasy when
               the wayside pulpit
               the open-windowed Jag
                     provide, provide
         '. . . gonna be OK, just . . .'

            dance past the posters girls

   come to our toy library
      come to our coffee morning
         come to our zumba keep-fit

            dole out the hymnbooks fawnsuit
the choir puff their cushions
      endorse peppermint air

               and someone will improvise a prayer
            if you party
         through that door

or with bottles waving arches
queue outside
the endangered public toilet
below *Happy Holidays* in neon

check those nose rings!
extemporise fawnsuit
on fleshly thorns
on pierced skin

scarlet lippy round the pews

fawnsuit pours Ribena into a goblet
'the blood of Christ'
for bodies soft as bread

Lynx mob vs. Brut gang
neo-Calvinist peashooters
humanist bollocks

to celebrate 'winterfest'
obliterate consciousness

add meaning
stripped down
to the least offensive point

a continuous period

extended ellipsis

[69]

Beach Mission

We carolled in caracoles on the sandbar.
Lotionees sprayed my tin with coin.
I toppled over a floppy breast.

Sunlounge attendants grew tentacles.
'Gods! Octopi!' the scaremongers
screamed from the observatory.

My backing choir of rabbits bared
transparencies of soul; solid
theology when eagles dived.

The scaremongers aimed prayers
as harpoons to octopi hearts.
The rabbits bobbed out of range.

Our sea psalms swallowed up
the rockpool electropop, a clam's
opening creak before the rook.

The rook's religion was the beak,
which chittered at the topless crew
carolling in caracoles on the sandbar.

Talent

Not a beauty, then, but still a singer, so no disappointment.
We found what we came to find, the prick of desire
waking us from what may have been years – like a dart
between the temples, the throw that earned a banning
from the local Guinness establishment decades ago –
and what have we made of them? The cinderhawk whistles,
it's up to our wood-smoked wrens to deliver. Of course,
they don't. The gutter press are leaning to a non-existent
sexual angle. Who shares the celebrity duvet? Liberal
journalists posit connections between ugliness and potential
talent that may one day be established, but for vespers
let us pray to a beautiful God – hair and beard shampooed
in 21st century toxins. No excuse when the attractive
fail like ginrats on a dungheap some hood has already
cleaned out. We check ourselves anxiously in mirrors.

The Boxer

'A two-legged dog hunting a new horizon of howls'

ROETHKE

The Boxer grunted like a sea lion and did tricks
with beach balls and rings until the fish
leapt for the back of his throat. In many ways,
mistakes can be made. Kate Moss mistook
the Prime Minister for a plumber because
he mentioned local floods, and now he's blocked
the flow of ideas between one aging pipe
dream and another. Kate Moss, the prophet,
unwelcome in her own town, which walked her
down the treadmill once or twice and thought
she'd never get off. Who would have thought?
Yes, mistakes can be made, alright. Unrequited
love entered my daily bowl of rations cleverly
disguised as Grace Kelly, a disco dancer
from Leeds whose name I never discovered
and a cultured Glaswegian mythologist
with wine-dark lips. I am cultivating a new
horizon of vineyards in hope that this world
isn't the end, that flower police will cultivate
religious vegetation. As long as I have two pipe
cleaner legs to carry me around, there's no harm
in pursuing my art. I have been working on
a lyric called The Boxer, a sort of Kate Moss
vs. Simon & Garfunkel growl mix, but it's really
about longings and other howlers I have made.

Horizontal

'The beams of our house are cedars: our rafters are firs.'

SONG OF SONGS 1: 17

The sawn-off gas pipe has a weakness
for human manoeuvre at ankle-level.

Cupboard doors stretch for skulls
to clatter. An identical crack

snaps at our heels like an argument
from room to room, trapdoor to trapdoor.

We crawl our way around by sound,
by stairwell croak and radiator drum,

negotiate grid north by the angle cut
between raindrops and the bedroom pail,

bow before the bulb's naked arc,
its wrecking ball swung among

bathroom tiles crumbling in extremes
of steam as we shower horizontally.

We try to occupy each space and tame
utilities as if contentment were a right

but drawers are full of tin openers,
cupboards empty of tin.

[73]

We bump heads beneath the wardrobe's
ringing hangers, and find ourselves

once more fresh out of love
for this house's clutter and bulk, the television

which seems least connected to a room
when switched on, the fridge

that leaks cold, the carbon monoxide fumes
we have learned to breathe

over six years, half a marriage and still
the rain breaches dark gaps

among beams and rafters, cedar and fir,
the concept of solidity

notional as a leakproof guarantee,
absurd as a silicone-plated heart.

We are brittle boned, arthritic jointed,
not stone frozen vertical for all weathers

in memorial for something forgotten.
Our love remains where we move from

or move to, resistant to our hopeless
DIY, our attempts to settle and stand.

Notes

The quotation from Yeats is from 'Prayer for my Daughter'.

Sunday Morning – the epigraph from Woody Allen can be found in his *Complete Prose* (Picador 1998)

An Angry Queen Tours the Royal Mile – the quoted lines in the middle of the poem are from Robert Fergusson's poem 'Auld Reikie' and are engraved beneath Ferguson's statue on the Royal Mile.

Locus-a-non: in certain European cities a few centuries ago, street sweepers would gather in the main squares at the end of each day to receive tips. The 'locus-a-non' tried to take advantage of this, as described in the poem.

A Scottish Cent(o)ury: the original inspiration for this poem came from Ian Pindar's cento, 'Chain Letter', in his collection *Emporium* (Carcanet 2011)

> L3, 'but greet . . . ' – but cry . . .
> L14, '. . .wha's licht slocks me' – . . . whose light extinguishes me
> L33, 'hits mizzerlessness, da marginalia, da element o winder' – its immeasurability, the marginalia, the element of wonder
> L84, 'Dinna be glaikit, dinna be ower smert' – don't be stupid, don't be too clever
> L85, '. . . tae a fremmit airt' – . . . to a peculiar direction
> L93, 'as we dat koort da storm's upstierin' – as we who court the storm's beginning

Generally, the lines and phrases are exactly those used in their original poems, but I have taken a few liberties with some of them for the sake of internal coherence, changing singular to plural, past to present, 'I' to 'we', 'the' to 'its', and vice-versa. I also felt free to add or subtract punctuation.

Sources: 1. Edwin Muir 'The Difficult Land'; 2. Valerie Gillies, 'We Meet Again'; 3. Hugh MacDiarmid 'The Bonnie Broukit Bairn'; 4. Joe Corrie, 'The Image o' God'; 5. William Soutar, 'The Permanence of the Young Men'; 6. Robert Garioch, 'Embro to the Ploy'; 7. William Montgomerie, 'Glasgow Street'; 8. Eleanor Livingstone, ' The Visit'; 9. Somhairle MacGill-Eain/Sorley Maclean, 'Hallaig'; 10. 'Iain Crichton Smith, 'Tonight'; 11. George Mackay Brown, 'Hamnavoe Market'; 12. C.F. Dutton, 'clach eanchainn'; 13. Alasdair Gray, 'Awakening'; 14. Christie Williamson, 'Gacela o da Flicht'; 15. Gael Turnbull, 'National Trust'; 16. Edwin Morgan, 'The Second Life; 17. W.S. Graham, 'The Nightfishing'; 18. Liz Lochhead, 'The Grim Sisters'; 19. Ivor Cutler, 'The Purposeful Culinary Implements'; 20. Ruaraidh MacThomais/Derick Thomson, 'Clann-Nighean an Sgadain'/'The Herring Girls'; 21. Peter McCarey, Tantris, part II; 22. Alexander Hutchison, 'An Ounce of Wit to a Pound of Clergy'; 23. Ian Abbot, 'Fishing through a Hole' 24. Andrew Greig, 'A Man is Driving'; 25. Andy Jackson, 'The Assassination Museum': 26. Eddie Gibbons, 'Eric Cantona Meets Frida Kahlo'; 27. Alasdair Paterson, 'On Nomenclature'; 28. W.N. Herbert, 'Hangover Thursday'; 29. John Burnside, 'Annunciation with a Garland of Self-Heal'; 30. Frank Kuppner, 'Arioflotga'; 31. Tim Turnbull, 'It Lives!'; 32. Polly Clark, 'My Life with Horses'; 33. Christine de Luca, 'Nae Aesy Mizzer'; 34. Robert Crawford, 'Crannog'; 35. Ron Butlin, 'At Linton Kirk'; 36. David Kinloch, 'Saltires'; 37. Nancy Somerville, 'The Big Hooley'; 38. Raymond Friel, 'Songs of the Plough'; 39. Meg Bateman, 'Lightness'; 40. Tom Leonard, 'The Voyeur'; 41. Brian McCabe, 'Seagull'; 42. Claire Askew, 'I'm sorry, I'm still in love with my grandmother'; 43. Tom Pow, 'Nebuchadnezzar in the Arboretum by Moonlight'; 44. Don Paterson, 'Prologue'; 45. Brian Johnstone, 'The Man Who Sang to Wine'; 46. Colin Will, 'Entering Your Poem'; 47. Vicki Feaver, 'Teddy Bears' 48. Mick Imlah, 'Goldilocks'; 49. Alan Gillis, 'Down Through Dark and Emptying Streets'; 50. Hugh McMillan, 'Leaving Scotland by Train'; 51. Ryan Van Winkle, 'Necessary Astronomy'; 52. Hazel Frew, 'Corridors'; 53. A.B. Jackson, 'Apocrypha, part II'; 54. Helena Nelson, 'From 'Interrogating the Silence''; 55. James MacGonigal, 'The Eye of the Beholder'; 56. Robin Robertson, 'Crossing the Archipelago'; 57. Martainn Mac An T-Saoir/Martin MacIntyre, 'Faces of a Uist Girl'; 58. Hamish Henderson, 'Second Elegy for the Dead in Cyrenaica': 59. Kei Miller, 'This Zinc Roof'; 60. Kevin Williamson, 'A Different Kind of Love'; 61. Gerry Loose, 'that person himself'; 62. Andrew Forster, 'Black Beauty'; 63. Alistair Findlay, 'Knox's Theory of Revolution'; 64. Lilias Scott Forbes, 'Turning a

Fresh Eye'; 65. John Glenday, 'For Lucie'; 66. Donald S. Murray, 'An Incomplete History of Rock Music in the Hebrides'; 67. Jen Hadfield, 'Towhee'; 68. James W. Wood, 'Byzantine'; 69. Norman MacCaig, 'Summer Farm'; 70. Sydney Goodsir Smith, 'Cokkils'; 71. Carol Ann Duffy, 'Prayer'; 72. Anna Crowe, 'The Pattern of our Days'; 73. Peter Manson, 'For January'; 74. Kathleen Jamie, 'The Queen of Sheba'; 75. Angus Calder, 'Haymarket Sunset'; 76. Jackie Kay, 'In My Country'; 77. Elizabeth Burns, 'The Stranger'; 78. Robin Fulton, 'It Takes a Rare Person'; 79. Richard Price, 'Like a Student Gardener'; 80. Sally Evans, 'Ullapool'; 81. Douglas Dunn, 'The Clear Day'; 82. Jim Carruth, 'A Cairn'; 83. Kate Clanchy, 'Timetable'; 84. James Robertson, 'A Manifesto for MSPs'; 85. Raymond Vettese, 'Prologue'; 86. Colin Herd, 'Cumbernauld'; 87. Margaret Christie, 'Suspended Animation'; 88. Jenni Daiches, 'Psalm'; 89. Andrew Philip, 'Notes to Self'; 90. Kapka Kassabova, 'How to Build Your Dream Garden'; 91. Dawn Wood, 'Her Grace'; 92. Cheryl Follon, 'Drinking Song'; 93. Robert Alan Jamieson, 'Kael-Jaerd'/'Kailyard'; 94. Stephen Nelson, 'The Vital Heart'; 95. J.L. Williams, 'History'; 96. Kona Macphee, 'Self-Portrait Aged 8 with Electric Fence'; 97. Ian Hamilton Finlay, 'Le Circus'; 98. Gerry Cambridge, 'A Winter Morning'; 99. Thomas A. Clarke, 'in the half-light of dusk . . .'; 100. Roddy Lumsden, 'A Story of Spice'.

Tippexed Speeches on Scottish Independence: I have subtracted, but not added, words from these speeches. All the same, they do not necessarily represent the views of those to whom they are attributed.

Thirteen: the Durs Grunbein epigraph comes from his 'Variations on No Theme' (in *Ashes for Breakfast*, Faber 2006), the form of which, slightly altered, I echo in this poem.

section iv.: some source material twisted from *Medieval Herbal Remedies: The Old English Herbarium and Anglo-Saxon Medicine* (5th century), translated by Anne van Arsdall.

section viii: source material culled and twisted from the following websites on depression - listverse.com/2007/11/21/top-10-tips-for-beating-depression/, masenka.be/category/mind-body/mind/depression/, ririanproject.com/2007/11/16/10-chemical-free-strategies-to-trick-yourself-out-of-the-blues/

section ix: the march in question was the Anti-Apartheid March from Glasgow to London, led by three former political prisoners, during Nelson Mandela's 25th year in prison.

Health Check: In Italy, GPs usually send pregnant mothers a document depicting their forthcoming children's chromosomes.

Torino in Furs: *Rai Due* is an Italian TV channel.

Beach Mission: the Wallace Stevens epigraph is from 'The Jack-Rabbit', from the collection, *Harmonium* (1922)

The Boxer: The epigraph from Roethke comes from his poem 'The Shape of Fire'.